Charles Woodruff Shields

Religion and Science in their Relation to Philosophy

An Essay on the present State of the Sciences

Charles Woodruff Shields

Religion and Science in their Relation to Philosophy
An Essay on the present State of the Sciences

ISBN/EAN: 9783337081454

Printed in Europe, USA, Canada, Australia, Japan

Cover: Foto ©ninafisch / pixelio.de

More available books at **www.hansebooks.com**

RELIGION AND SCIENCE.

RELIGION AND SCIENCE

IN THEIR RELATION TO

PHILOSOPHY.

AN ESSAY ON THE PRESENT STATE OF THE SCIENCES.

Read before the Philosophical Society of Washington.

BY
CHARLES W. SHIELDS, D. D.,
PROFESSOR OF THE HARMONY OF SCIENCE AND REVEALED RELIGION,
IN PRINCETON COLLEGE, N. J.

NEW YORK:
SCRIBNER, ARMSTRONG, AND COMPANY.
1875.

Entered, according to Act of Congress, in the year 1875, by
SCRIBNER, ARMSTRONG, AND COMPANY,
In the Office of the Librarian of Congress, at Washington.

RIVERSIDE, CAMBRIDGE:
STEREOTYPED AND PRINTED BY
H. O. HOUGHTON AND COMPANY.

PREFATORY NOTE.

THE following essay was prepared originally as a paper to be read before the Philosophical Society of Washington, under the title of "The Present State of the Sciences," and with the understanding that it would traverse in a philosophical spirit the ground occupied by the recent Address of Dr. Tyndall to the British Association at Belfast.

Numerous requests for it in a more permanent form having been received since its publication by the "New York Tribune" for November the 7th ult., the author has taken the opportunity to revise it and insert some additional matter which could not be brought within the limits of the original occasion. No attempt, however, has been made to unfold the themes presented, as it is his hope to treat of them in an extended work, projected since the year 1860, and designed to exhibit the Harmony of Science and Revealed Religion as fundamental and preliminary to the Final Philosophy or Theory of Perfectible Science.

PRINCETON COLLEGE, *February*, 1875.

PROCEEDINGS OF THE PHILOSOPHICAL SOCIETY OF WASHINGTON.

Prof. JOSEPH HENRY, LL. D., President, in the Chair.

At a meeting of the Philosophical Society of Washington, held October 24th, 1874, a paper was read by the Rev. Dr. C. W. Shields of Princeton College, "On the Present State of the Sciences."

On motion the thanks of the Society were presented to Rev. Dr. Shields, and the hope was expressed that his essay might be widely circulated. — *Extract from the Minutes.*

J. H. C. COFFIN, *Secretary.*

THE PRESENT STATE OF THE SCIENCES.

It should be premised that this essay will embrace but a small part of an immense field. It can claim to be nothing more than a mere glimpse of the existing state of the sciences from a philosophical point of view, and will simply aim to bring forward certain general principles which are believed to be already latent in many thoughtful minds and of special interest at the present time.

On a careful review of the history of the sciences, it could be shown that each of them, since the Reformation, has broken into two sections, the one mainly scientific and the other largely religious, and that these two sections, in parting from each other, have proceeded through three distinct stages, more or less successive and chronological. The first might be termed a stage of healthful separation and progress, marked by ascertained facts and truths; the second, a stage of mutual avoidance, filled with various hypotheses and dogmas; and the third, a stage of open rupture, issuing in antagonistic speculations and creeds. It would be interesting to test this generalization by tracing the sciences from one stage to another during the last three centuries, together with the discoveries, opinions, and controversies which have marked their career. Indeed it is plain that without some such review of the past growth of knowledge, we can neither understand its present state nor forecast its future progress. The history of the sciences can alone lead us to what Whewell and Comte have termed their philosophy — that Science of the Sciences which the sciences themselves must yield as their last and noblest fruitage. On this occasion, however, some acquaintance with such history may be assumed, and it will be enough to present the results which have been drawn from it, and leave them to stand upon their own evidence.

Let us define the field before us. Leaving out of view those portions of knowledge which have attained to scientific certainty and are no longer in debate, those discovered facts and laws which alone make positive science, we shall find remaining to be considered a mass of unsolved problems, mostly questions of origin and destiny, which are growing more complex every hour, and before which the religious and scientific champions of our day are now crossing lances, like the two knights before the mystic shield, with their respective dogmas and hypotheses in a more or less contradictory state. It will be our first task to survey the opposite sides or phases of these questions as expressed in such dogmas and hypotheses, from an independent point of view, in a strictly philosophical mood, with an effort to do each of them the utmost justice. We shall then have the materials for a full and fair decision.

ASTRONOMICAL PROBLEMS.

Astronomy — to begin with the oldest of the concrete sciences — still offers to the two parties that ever present problem which has tasked our race for thousands of years, the origin of the heavens, the production of those mysterious bodies, the sun, planets, and satellites, the stars, galaxies, and nebulæ which fill the immensity of space around us. On the one side of this question we have the hypothesis of universal evolution, of the spontaneous growth of worlds out of crude matter by means of its own laws from an indefinite antiquity and immensity; in a word, the rise of the present cosmos from a former chaos. It is an hypothesis as old as the days of Leucippus, Democritus, and Epicurus, who held that the original atoms, struggling together throughout space and time, have at last, after infinite trials, brought forth the existing worlds as the fittest to survive their mazy conflict. And though it slumbered during the early and middle ages, until it was revived by Bruno, Gassendi, and others, in the seventeenth century, it has since come forth again with renewed vigor and in still more scientific forms. Descartes led the way, devoutly assuring the Sorbonne that the worlds were no doubt created perfect, while, nevertheless, he would show how they might have arisen on mechanical principles from certain vortices or vast eddies of different matter forming and whirling the sun and planets like boats in a maelstrom. Leibnitz, in place of the vortices, put the monads or living atoms acting and reacting under preëstablished harmonics until they evolved the present solar system as the best possible world. Immanuel Kant, applying the physics of Newton, sketched a natural history of the celestial bodies as at first massed out of a stormy chaos of attractive and repulsive particles, then formed into revolving globes, and finally poised in the equilibrium of the planetary forces. Laplace at length completed such views with his magnificent postulate of a primitive nebula, or universal fire-mist, eddying into a central igneous body like the sun, breaking into rotating rings such as those of Saturn, cooling into cloudy and watery spheres such as Jupiter and Neptune, and at last hardening into solid shells such as that which incrusts the fiery core of our earth. The elder Herschel pushed this sublime speculation with the telescope beyond our solar firmament into the sidereal heavens, where he detected, as he supposed, vast nebulous masses with lucid points glittering as the nuclei of new worlds, or rather of ancient worlds so remote that ages must yet pass ere the tardy light can paint their finished form in the eye of man. Humboldt, in view of such researches, grandly described the whole celestial spectacle as only in appearance simultaneous, having beyond it an endless perspective of stars and galaxies too distant to be portrayed as yet in other than their embryo stages, as mere films and dots of light. Other authorities still living might be cited who hold or use the same hypothesis, and it is now claimed that the spectroscope has raised it to the rank of a theory by exhibiting in the chemical constitution of different stars all the successive phases of cosmic growth, nebula, sun, and planet, as plainly bursting into life throughout the heavens, as the germ, leaf, and flower at our feet.

On the other side of the question we have the dogma of immediate creation, of an instantaneous starting forth of the heavens and earth from nothing in their present form, at the mere word of Jehovah. It is a dogma which claims to be as old as the Hebrew and Christian Scriptures, and in various terms has been formulated and handed down to us by the rabbis, the fathers, the schoolmen, the reformers, and the divines of the following age. Philo, the Platonic Jew, in agreement with the Maccabees, held that the worlds were not formed from anything preëxistent, but spoken into being from nothing. Clement of Alexandria, in opposition to the Epicureans, delighted to represent the creation of the universe as a voluntary act of Divine love. Augustine more precisely taught that the Deity fashioned the heavens and earth not out of matter, nor yet out of himself, but out of nothing, by an instaneous exertion of His own free will. Aquinas followed with the scholastic distinction that God from eternity willed that the world should be, and not that the world should be from eternity — that He created with it both space and time, and that He was the author of matter rather than its mere former. Melancthon, in contrast with the Stoical notion of eternal matter, designated the creative act as a simple fiat, commanding things to be which had not been before. Calvin stigmatized as a profane jeer the inquiry why the heavens and earth should have been created only six thousand years ago, after so many idle ages had rolled away and with so much vacant space left running to waste. The great body of living divines following these different authorities in the Jewish, Greek, Roman Catholic, and Protestant Churches, still teach or confess the same dogma, and at this hour, while the telescope and spectroscope are disclosing unnumbered worlds throughout infinite space and time, it stands defined in the same terms as when the heavens were but admired as a blue canopy or a spangled vault.

Let it here be noted, once for all, that the hypotheses and dogmas which are held respecting scientific questions are now coming before us in their pure and simple form, without any admixture with each other, and as enunciated by the highest authorities. Among astronomers, as well as divines, it need scarcely be said, may be found many, such as the elder Herschel and Stephen Alexander, who seek to blend the theory of evolution with the doctrine of creation in their cosmogonic speculations, as well as some, such as Laplace and Humboldt, who would put them apart or at variance; but such classes do not now come within this survey.

Besides the origin of the heavens, the question of their destiny, so long a mere theme of devout fancy, is becoming also a problem of exact science. It was taught by all the great doctors, poets, and artists, from the days of Clement, Bernard, and Michael Angelo, that the whole existing firmament might at any moment be destroyed and renewed by the flames of a general conflagration in order to become the pure abode of saints and angels; and even since the rise of astronomical conceptions, the comet, the meteor, and the aurora have ever and anon been hailed as portents of judgment and signs of the approaching kingdom of heaven. But we are now assured, on the authority of leading physicists, such as Grove, Helmholtz, and Tyndal, that so far as science can yet foresee, the advancing evolution can only issue in gradual dissolution; that the potential forces of heat, light, and life, which have been stored from the primitive nebula, or from surrounding meteors in star, sun, and planet, as the ages roll on, will inevitably be spent, and the whole machinery of the heavens fall back into ruins; that already the moon is but a charred cinder of the earth, the earth a cooling ember of the sun, the sun a blazing fragment of the stars, the stars themselves but dying suns, and all their galaxies doomed to pale and wane into universal night and death.

The design of the heavens, the habitability of other worlds and their mutual relations, the possibility of life and intelligence throughout the universe, are also emerging questions of like double import. While the one party, from Dionysius and Gregory to Chalmers, have imagined an ascending hierarchy of angels, principalities, and powers, rank above rank, through the heaven of heavens toward the throne of Jehovah; the other party, from Plutarch and Galileo to Whewell, can discern in the stars, sun, and planets only so many globes of fire, vapor, and slag, wholly incapable of sustaining life and reason, and as destitute of any intelligible purpose as the crystals that sparkle or the flowers that bloom where no eye can ever see them.

And the concluding question as to the goal or aim of the whole cosmic process has at length issued in the extreme opinions of Jonathan Edwards and Herbert Spencer; on the one hand that of a miraculous creation and regeneration of the heavens and earth at fixed epochs for the good of creatures and the glory of their Creator; on the other hand, that of a rhythmic ebb and flow of ever persistent force from nebula to planet and planet to nebula, from chaos to cosmos and cosmos to chaos, through endless cycles of evolving and dissolving worlds, amid which man sports upon the earth, as the merest animalcule of a bubble that flashes in the sunshine.

GEOLOGICAL PROBLEMS.

Geology next meets us with problems scarcely less grand and even more interesting, such as the origin of our own planet, the formation of the rocky layers which inclose its hidden contents, and the growth of the fossil plants and animals which are found buried in its crust. On the one side of the question is the hypothesis of secular evolution, of a slow unfolding of the globe from a chaotic mass into its organized form through the action of existing causes during indefinite time. If any germs of such an hypothesis can be traced in the mundane egg of Orpheus and Aristophanes, the primitive water and fire of Thales and Heraclitus, and the speculations of Strabo upon floods and volcanoes, they remained buried under dogmatic traditions during the Middle Ages until they were again brought forth by the early Italian geologists, as Lyell has shown, and at length cast into a more scientific shape. Leibnitz, without calling in question the Mosaic cosmogony, postulated for his "protogea" or primitive earth, a sort of extinguished sun, slowly cooling through fire and vapor into the clouds, seas, lands, and strata of our present globe. Buffon, at the request of the Theological Faculty, recanted a similar "Theory of the Earth," in which he had fancied the planets as ancient fragments of the sun, struck off by a comet and left freezing as they whirled in their orbits; our earth at this date still retaining the volcanic nucleus and universal ocean by whose joint action its seas and continents are formed. Werner and Hutton, as founders of the rival schools of Neptunists and Vulcanists, at length traced the aqueous and igneous strata to the same causes which are still producing alluvium and lava, though at a rate that would require an immeasurable past. Lamarck and St. Hilaire broached theories of transmutation serving to blend together through long epochs the fossil and living species which Cuvier would have broken apart with his successive deluges. Herschel and Poisson, in like manner, sought to transform ancient into modern climates by means of celestial causes of inconceivable slowness, such as a swaying of the earth's orbit and poles in the solar rays, a fluctuation of heat and light in the sun itself, and even radiation among the stars. Babbage and Lyell traced the secular changes of climate and species to more terrestrial causes, such as the decline of the earth's primitive heat and the gradual shifting of the continents by the action of its crust. Humboldt, bringing these facts together in one comprehensive review, has sketched the progressive stages of our planet as at first a fiery ring cast off from the nebulous sun, then an incandescent sphere, and at length a granite shell sustaining between the central fire and solar heat the successive kingdoms of organic life which for unknown ages have flourished upon its surface. Most living geologists and palæontologists seem to proceed upon some such hypothesis; and by the advanced party, according to Professor Huxley, it is held to be not unlikely that the whole development of the globe through all its eras and phases may yet be as plainly traced as the growth of a fowl within the egg.

On the other side of the same question is the dogma of successive creations, of Almighty fiats calling into being one after another, land and sea and sky, reptiles, plants, and animals, in six days of twenty-four hours, a few thousand years ago. Although derived from the Mosaic Genesis, it is a dogma which has varied its terms with each age of the Church. The early fathers, Clement and Origen, treated the six days as sacred allegories rather than literal epochs. The later fathers, Athanasius and Augustine, termed them the mere timeless acts of an instantaneous creation, successive only in our thought, and figuratively represented to us as working days measured by sunrise and sunset. The schoolmen, Hugh of St. Victor and Peter Lombard, defined them as miraculous works which might indeed have been performed all at once as the fathers taught, but in fact were produced successively in six literal days as religious lessons of the Creator to his creatures. The Westminster divines also held them to be periods of twenty-four hours, and found their rationale in the seven-fold division of time in six days of work with one of worship. Francis Turretine argued that each day's work was produced instantaneously by a single fiat, plants and animals starting forth in a mature state and therefore in the autumn of the year. Archbishop Usher, by act of Parliament, fixed the date of Creation on the 25th of October, 4004, B. C. The learned Dr. Gill particularized the name as well as date of each creative day from Monday morning to Saturday night. Living divines who still follow these different authorities have as yet made no new definitions of the dogma, and for anything that appears in our existing creeds, the interminable strata, floras, and faunas which geologists have been unfolding, are still to be viewed as only so many didactic miracles wrought in a single week.

As before indicated, it would not fall within the scope of this survey to notice the more scientific attempts of Hugh Miller and Guyot to expand still further the Mosaic days into vast creative epochs or cosmogonic eras; nor yet the less dogmatic efforts of Strauss and

Baden Powell to resolve them into a philosophic myth or poem.

The destiny of the globe is also becoming a scientific as well as a religious question. It formed part of the ancient faith as matured by Augustine and Aquinas and depicted in the sacred arts, that our earth, having once been cleansed by water for the sin of man, would yet be purged by fire for his redemption, at a given signal when the Purgatory beneath it would send forth its flames. And even some of the early geologists, such as Hooke and Ray, looked upon the earthquake and the volcano as agents, no less than presages, of such a catastrophe. But we are now told in accordance with the views of Fourier, Thompson, and Mayer, that the earth is already oxidated or burnt through its crust halfway to the core; that it has grown so cool in the course of ages that it could not now melt a layer of ice ten feet thick in one hundred years; and that the lunar tides which act as brakes upon the rotatory motion imparted by its primordial heat must in time cause it to spin more slowly and feebly, until at length it shall flutter upon its axis as a dead world like the moon, ever turning the same pallid face to the sun.

And the remaining question as to the end or scope of the whole terrestrial development, at length lands us between the contrasted views of Burnet and Lyell; on the one side that of a miraculous deluge and conflagration of the earth between the epochs of creation and judgment, for the sake of man alone; and on the other side that of vast periodic changes of climate and species as the globe heaves and shifts its continents and seas through the great year of the zodiac, or nods to and from the sun, crowned with verdure and capped with snow every other 12,000 years, or mayhap journeys with the sun itself among the stars 18,000,000,000 years through a sidereal summer and winter, between which our whole historic era with all its growing annals and splendid works shall seem transient as the hues of morning or the flowers of spring.

PROBLEMS OF ANTHROPOLOGY.

Anthropology at this point comes forward with problems still more complex and momentous, such as the origin of our race, the first appearance of man upon the earth, and the mode of his connection with the organic scale. On the one side of the question rises before us the hypothesis of derivative evolution, of a gradual growth of animal into human species, under organic and climatic laws, long ages ere history was born. It was a prevalent opinion of the ancient Greeks and Romans, as expressed by Epicurus and Horace, that when the animals of the new earth at first crept forth as a dumb and filthy herd, they fought for acorns and hiding-places with their fists, with cudgels, at length with weapons; that soon they invented names for things and words for their thoughts, and finally began to abstain from war, to fortify towns, and to enact laws. But since this classic myth disappeared from the view of Western Europe before the traditions of the Church, it has only been by successive conquests over physical and religious antipathy, that the grim pleasantries of Monboddo and Samuel Johnson have at length passed into a grave controversy of science. De Maillet, vailing his ironical purpose in a "Dialogue between a Christian Missionary and a Heathen Sage," opened the question with glimpses of the primitive animals, the merman among them, rising from the slime of the Deluge and becoming in the course of generations adapted to the slowly desiccated earth. Lamarck imagined such transmutations to have occurred through the long eras and stages of an organic progression by the instinctive efforts of animals to adjust themselves to new conditions, the stranded turtle growing into the tortoise, the high-browsing camel into the giraffe, and even the upright orang into savage and civilized man. The author of the "Vestiges of Creation" recalled these speculations from the obscurity into which they had been shaded by the great name of Cuvier, mainly to show the need of some higher law of development than the mere efforts and habits of animals themselves. Professor Richard Owen many years ago surmised the probable action of a physical law by which nature has advanced, with slow and stately steps, through the archetypal light, from the earliest vertebrate in the fish, to the glorious form of man. Messrs. Darwin, Hooker, and Wallace have at length proposed as such a law for the vegetable and animal world the survival of the best or fittest breeds in the struggle for subsistence which is ever going on among the teeming populations of nature. Mr. Darwin, conjecturing that man himself may thus have fought his way upward from the inferior races, has been collecting the inherited proofs of such origin from his embryonic stages, his rudimental organs, and his very physiognomy. Professor Huxley has suggested that even his highest faculties of feeling and intellect may be seen germinating in some of the lower species with which he is most nearly connected. Professor Haeckel declares that, in the course of his organic life, from the germ to the grave, he epitomizes all the successive types of the palæontological scale. And Sir Charles Lyell already looks for his pedigree in the entombed dynasties of nature among such typical shapes as the proudest nobles still blazon for their crests. It is frequently said that the majority of living naturalists accept the hypothesis in its different forms, or at least the principle upon which it proceeds, and they would doubtless agree with a saying attributed to Schaaffhausen, that the secular transformation of animal into human species, if once proved, could be no more marvelous to science than the simplest metamorphosis of an egg into a bird or of a child into a man.

On the other side of the same question stands the dogma of independent creation, of an immediate formation of man out of the ground, in the image of God, on the sixth day of the first week of the world. It has come down to us through various forms of statement, from the earliest comments on the writings of Moses. The rabbins, from the son of Sirach to Philo, delighted to depict the divine image in Adam as reflecting every conceivable perfection of body and mind. The fathers Tertullian, Chrysostom, and Augustine discerned it in his godlike aspect and dominion, in his intellectual and moral attributes, and in a miniature trinity of his body, soul, and spirit. The schoolmen, St. Bernard, Lombard, and Duns Scotus distinguished it into that intellectual image which even in Gehenna cannot be consumed, and that moral likeness which he lost by the fall. The later doctors Bellarmin and Suarez described such moral likeness as a paradisaic dowry which he had forfeited, a virginal wreath of which he had been despoiled. The reformers Luther and Calvin, the Puritans Owen and Edwards, redefined it as a physical, intellectual, and moral likeness which has been wholly lost or marred, and can only be supernaturally restored. No existing body of divines has since thought of retouching these ancient symbols, and at the present moment, while anthropologists on all sides are mining into the fossil flora and fauna coeval with primitive man, our reigning dogmatic conceptions are still as crude and vague as the frescoes of Raphael and the paradise of Milton.

It will be observed that the pre-Adamite and co-Adamite races of Peyrerius and Agassiz, as well as the pre-lapsarian tribes of Büchner and Vogt, by the terms of our survey, are alike excluded from view.

The development of mankind, the rise of races, languages, and arts is a further question which science begins to share with religion. It has been the traditional faith, from the time of Augustine, that the human species, being potentially folded in Adam, fell with him from Paradise, became whelmed in a universal flood, were renewed from the loins of Noah, and afterward, by a miraculous confusion of language, dispersed over the earth into nations and tribes, with an ever-lapsing or perverted civilization. And until very lately, scientific anthropologists were retracing all existing races to Shem, Ham, and Japhet; all living dialects to the primitive Hebrew, and all remaining monuments and traditions to the tower of Babel. But we are now threatened with a total revolution of these opinions. Ethnologists, such as Agassiz, Morton, and Owen, have been grouping mankind into indigenous races, through all the hues of climate, from the Ethiopian sable to the rose of Circassia; grading them in distinct classes, by all degrees of the facial angle, from the low forehead of the ape to the vertical brow of the Apollo; and following them backward from one epoch to another beyond the time of Moses, through all the dynasties of the Pharaohs. Philologists such as Max Müller, Whitney, and Schleicher, have been unfolding human speech into its formative stages, the radical, the agglutinate, the amalgamate; tracing its roots to imitative sounds or natural cries, and even expanding its growth through long eras of fossil dialects, rudimentary letters, and phonetic types, between the extremes of animal and human expression, from the chatter of an Australian forest to the comedies of Shakespeare and Molière. Archæologists, such as Lubbock, Stevens, and Westropp, have been sketching human culture through its pre-historic ages of stone, of bronze, and of iron, from the flint-chip to the steam-engine, from the rude cairn to the marbles of the Parthenon, and exhibiting the savage peoples of the earth in advancing stages, the hunter, the herdsman, the farmer, during long epochs, ere civilization was known. And archæo-geologists, so called, such as Schmerling, Lartet, and Lyell, have been restoring the flora and fauna of the pre-historic periods, the beech and the horse of the iron age, the oak and the goat of the bronze age, the pine and the reindeer of the stone age, the bear and the glacier of the savage epoch, until at last they have carried the torch into a primeval cavern, in search of mammoth bones and simian skulls, as the rude birthplace of civilized man.

And the concluding question as to the destiny of mankind, the aim and prospect of the whole human evolution, at length opens two opposite views; on the one side, the prediction of a regenerated race upon the scene of a renovated earth, with the wilderness budding as a rose, the lion transformed into a lamb, and man again an innocent child of paradise; and on the other side, the prognosis of a gradual decline as well as growth of humanity, when the noblest races shall have lost their ancestral vigor, the richest tongues their classic grace, the finest arts their pristine purity; when even the productive stores and sustaining powers of nature herself shall have been exhausted, and the lingering plants, animals, and effete tribes of men shall fade away like the leaves of Autumn, while the earth veers back into her glacial epoch, and the sun can no longer vivify the nations that have basked in his rays.

PROBLEMS IN THE PSYCHICAL SCIENCES.

Our survey has now brought us to the verge of those higher psychical sciences which, as they include the nearest human interests, are bristling with portentous questions, not likely to be treated in that passionless mood which belongs to scientific inquiries, and yet all the more imperiously claiming our attention.

Psychology is already pressing upon us such problems as the origin, the development and the destiny of the individual, of his cognitions, his emotions, his volitions, and is presenting like divergent opinions; on the one side such recent hypotheses as those of Herbert Spencer, Maudsley, and Moleschott, that mind is a product of matter, that the will is a developed force acting under laws, and that death is the dissolution of that matter, the conversion of that force; and on the other side, such traditional dogmas as those of Lactantius, Augustine, and Jerome, that the soul has been created in the body, that the will may be regenerated by irresistible grace, and that the spirit will be reclothed hereafter with the whole present body. And while some psychologists are ready to retrace the devout materialism of Bonnet and Priestley, others are but reverting to the sensual fatalism of La Mettrie and D'Holbach.

Sociology is not far behind with such problems as the origin, the development, and the destiny of society, of its arts, its sciences, its polities; and is branching with a similar divergence of views; on the one side, the hypotheses of such civilians as Locke, Vico, and Draper, that the state is a social contract; that the history of nations proceeds under periodic and progressive laws, and that societies, like individuals, physiologically viewed, have their infancy, youth, age, and decline, are born but to grow and die ; and on the other side, the dogmas of such ecclesiastics as Bellarmin, Bossuet, and Edwards, that the church is an absolute theocracy, that Providence throughout history has been a systematic judgment of the nations on behalf of the church, and that the nations are yet to be subdued by the miraculous return and reign of Christ. And if some scientific historians, like Buchez and Patrick

Dove, have looked for their ideal society in the course of prophecy and Providence, others, like Condorcet and St. Simon, have sought it only through revolution and reform.

Theology also is emerging with new problems, such as the origin, the development, and the destiny of religion, of its traditions, its creeds, and its cults, and is already breaking into hostile camps; on the one side, the votaries of mere natural religion, such as Theodore Parker, Max Müller, and Comte, holding that there is one essential universal faith derived from the light of nature, that there has been a scale and growth of religions in history through degrees of relative perfection, and that the perfect religion of the future will consist in the deification of humanity, the worship of womanhood, and the hierarchy of science; and on the other side, the disciples of revealed religion, such as Leland, Paley, and Chalmers, maintaining that a revelation of religion is necessary as well as important; that there has been a primitive miraculous revelation, of which other pretended revelations are but corruptions or counterfeits, and that this revealed religion is destined to prevail over all other religions by supernatural conversions and judgments at the end of the present dispensation. And though some comparative theologians, such as Hardwick and Edward Spiess, are endeavoring to

THE PRESENT STATE OF THE SCIENCES. 31

recapitulate the world's religions in Christianity, others, such as Strauss and Feuerbach, have striven to reduce Christianity itself to mere mythology and self-illusion. And the general question to be gathered from all the psychical sciences at length presents to us on the one side the opinion that the regenerate soul, the church, and the coming millennium are parts of a new spiritual system ensuing upon the old material creation, and on the other side the conjecture that religion, science, politics, art, all were once potential in the flames of the sun, and must yet revert to the fiery cloud from whence they sprang.

PROBLEMS OF METAPHYSICAL SCIENCE.

Behind these problems of the physical and psychical sciences are others still more recondite and abstruse — the metaphysical questions as to the essential nature of mind and matter and the absolute reality before and beneath all phenomena; questions which on the one side have at length issued in the opinions of Herbart, Lotze, and Fechner that phenomena both material and spiritual are the expressions of real essences or conscious monads, or self-manifesting souls; together with the extreme speculations of Hegel, Schopenhauer, and Hartmann, that the intelligible universe is a logical process of absolute reason and thought, or a product of blind primordial force and human will, or a historical development of unconscious force and will into conscious thought and reason. Questions which, on the other side, have scarcely advanced beyond the ancient dogmas, that body and soul are created substances co-acting mechanically as instruments of divine foreordination, and that there is a trinity of Father, Son, and Spirit in the self-existent Jehovah manifested to us through the miracles of creation, incarnation, atonement, and final judgment.

At the same time, as the issue of modern metaphysical thought, we have at the one extreme an optimism which seeks to identify the revealed Jehovah as the one Absolute Reason, the first and final cause of a perfected creation; and at the other extreme a pessimism which would exhibit the developing universe as an abortive paradox, beginning and ending in hopeless contradiction.

PROBLEMS IN THE SCIENCE OF SCIENCES.

And high above all these problems in the different sciences, we may now behold the great summary question as to the course and goal of the sciences themselves, as to their logical processes, their historical laws, and their ultimate limits. On the one side we have the decisions of Bacon, D'Alembert, Comte, Mill, and Spencer, that positive 'science is restricted to facts and their laws without inquiring into their first and final causes, that the more advanced sciences have historically reached this positive state only by excluding all inquiry into causes, and thus outgrowing and destroying theology and metaphysics, and that their final goal is sheer nescience or the recognition of an unknowable reality as the ground of all knowable phenomena. On the other side we have the opinions of Tertullian, Aquinas, Calvin, and Butler, that the unknowable to man is revealed by God through miraculously attested communications, that it has been the function of such revelation to remedy human ignorance and expose false science, and that ultimately all earthly science for the individual will be lost in beatific vision, and for the race will be eclipsed by the millennial light of a new apocalypse. And it remains to be seen whether, in the true theory of science, reason is to progressively coincide with revelation, or revelation to be gradually superseded by reason.

Such then is the present state of the sciences. While they embrace immense bodies of exact knowledge, too vast for any one mind to master, too magnificent for even the imagination to depict, they also present a bewildering mass of unsolved problems with opposite hypotheses and dogmas respecting them which have been held by the master-spirits of former times, and which still engross the leading intellects of our day. Renewing the remark with which this paper began, that the aim has been simply to state these questions with all fairness and not to discuss them, I shall now submit some deductions from the survey which seem to lie upon the surface in full view of all parties.

PHILOSOPHICAL NATURE OF THESE PROBLEMS.

In the first place, it is plain that these questions are not purely scientific. They have not been so treated in past ages, and they are not so treated at the present day. No competent scientific authority has yet pronounced upon them. The French Academy has not decided them. The British Association has not decided them. The different Italian, German, and American associations have not decided them. There is not even any spontaneous concurrence of scientific men respecting them, such as that which attends all observed facts, ascertained laws, and proved theories. It cannot be claimed that the great names in science have ever been or are now, arrayed against the religious view of them. And it is not too much to say that they can never be decided by any merely scientific process. The origin and destiny of nebulæ, suns, and planets, of man with his individual, social, and religious interests, of the universe through all its eras and phases, are surely problems which by no inductive search among existing facts and laws, can be fully brought within the revision and prevision of science, but must sooner or later, as her most loyal votaries are now confessing, lead her to that verge of the knowable where her torch becomes quenched in the Unknowable and she has no more light to shed.

In the second place, it is also clear that these questions are not merely religious. If they were so treated in former times, they are not so treated to-day. The religious authorities which have ventured to pronounce upon them have not settled them. The Papal Syllabus has not settled them. The Evangelical Alliance has not settled them. The different ecclesiastical councils have not settled them. There is not even such general agreement of religious people concerning them as that which belongs to the chief essentials of the Christian faith. It cannot be held that the great names in religion have always been or are now joined together against the scientific view of them. And it is safe to say that by no purely religious method can they ever be settled. The attempt of all churches and sects combined, through any mere grammatic interpretation of the Holy Scriptures, under pretense of infallible guidance, and in contempt of all other means of knowledge, to show how the heavens and earth and man were created and will be renewed, would simply remand religion to the superstition and bigotry of the dark ages, and at length, as her most devout disciples will admit, dim her light at the very points where it should shine most brightly.

In the third place, it will follow that these questions, being partly scientific and partly religious, are strictly philosophical, and should be so treated by all parties. That they are partly scientific and partly religious is a fact that runs through all the past. From their very origin they have involved both elements. The history of neither could be written without that of the other. The successive conflicts and alliances of the scientific and religious classes at the great epochs of civilization, among the Sophists, among the Fathers, among the Schoolmen, among the Reformers, have been the very rythm of human progress. There is scarcely a dogma which has not served as an hypothesis in science, as there is scarcely an hypothesis which has not been used for a dogma in religion. The great names in each, or at least the masters in both, have ever striven to keep them together rather than to drive them apart. Plato and Origen, Augustine and Erigena, Albertus and Roger Bacon, Francis Bacon and Butler, from age to age, have illustrated their essential oneness. It could be shown, indeed, as the largest minds on both sides have long perceived, that their own peculiar processes and exigencies soon bring them face to face in the mutual recognition of knowable facts which the one must discover and of unknowable realities which the other must reveal. And the common ground between them, formed by their intersection, instead of narrowing has been enlarging with the lapse of time and the growth of knowledge, until now it has become not merely a conspicuous arena in the philosophical world, but even a popular sign of the times.

PROFESSOR TYNDALL'S ILLUSTRATION.

Of this fact there could scarcely have been a more striking proof than the recent brilliant and lucid address of Professor Tyndall from the chair of the British Association — an address widely and justly praised, as well for the graces of its style as for the vigor, acuteness, and breadth of its thought, the elevation, courage, and candor of its tone. That the questions which it broaches could be so discussed and received in a scientific body, would be a full vindication, were any needed, of their fitness to such occasions. It was right that they should be taken there, and it is right that they should be brought here, if only they are held under the dry light of pure science, within the purview of philosophy. How to adjust them has indeed become "the problem of problems at the present hour;" and that, not merely that we may "yield reasonable satisfaction to a religious sentiment in the emotional nature," for with this, science may have little to do; but also, and chiefly, that we may meet a logical demand of the understanding, a crowning want of the intellect of man.

Perhaps the true philosophical nature of the problems which have been stated could not be better illustrated, for the present purpose at least, than by means of the rhetorical device so skillfully employed in that paper. A disciple of Lucretius, it will be remembered, is supposed to have engaged Bishop Butler in an encounter of wits over one of the chapters in his immortal Analogy; the combatants having been armed with the added knowledge of our time, like Milton's embattled angels, to dare an argument of mysteries. It is easy to paint portraits to suit ourselves when we hold the pencil, and there is always some risk of unfairness in speaking for another. But I shall try to avoid such dangers as my predecessor has done, by simply fancying the two disputants to reappear before us at the point which their discussion had reached, and allowing them to proceed with it, in our hearing, a step further toward its logical issue. Let the Bishop speak first, and the disciple of Lucretius shall have the last word.

" Before we leave this subject of living agents, most noble Lucretian, I beg to remind you that there is involved in it a very interesting question which you have scarcely touched upon. You will remember that my whole argument had reference not so much to the nature of the living agent or self, as to its destiny. I was trying to prove inductively, from observed facts, that our survival after death is as probable, if not as certain, as any other scientific prevision attempted under like conditions. Beginning with those two great presumptions or high probabilities upon which all positive science proceeds, the uniformity and continuance of nature, I argued that we shall continue to live hereafter, unless it be imagined that death, of which we know nothing, destroys us; and against this mere imaginary presumption I brought forward various scientific presumptions afforded by observation and experience, such as the following: That if death means, as you affirm, the dissolution of your atoms, then your essential bulk may be such that you cannot be dissolved, like that infinitesimal germ out of which has been developed your whole present self, together with the inherited traits of your ancestors: That already most of your atoms have been dissolved and replaced every seven, ten, or twenty years, not merely bones, tissues, nerves, but the brain itself, dying a thousand deaths: That large portions even of your nervous atoms might be dissolved without being replaced and you still be conscious of your phantom-limb, or go on thinking with but half of your brain : That through all these dissolutions, that hidden self of yours, picture it as you will, persists and survives, with its peculiar powers of thought and feeling, whatever they may be, even amid disease, injury, and madness itself: That after the last more rapid dissolution, sooner or later, should that mysterious consciousness, of which you have spoken as coming and going so strangely, be recovered in some new ethereal organism as unlike its old counterpart as that god-like form was itself unlike its earlier icthyic germ, or as the brilliant insect is unlike its off-cast larva, some spiritual body,[1] wholly imperceptible by our present senses, yet itself gifted with more than microscopic insight, locomotive swiftness, and telegraphic thought — all these marvels would be no greater than are daily passing before your eyes: That though existing plants and animals, having shown no such power of individual progression, should

---

[1] Carpenter's *Human Physiology*, Art. 78.

perish with their species and be replaced by other and fitter forms in that second state into which you had been born —

  "'With all the circle of the wise,
   The perfect flower of human time,'

yet even this would be only such meet survival as now separates us from primeval ferns and dragons, a just predominance of the higher over the lower forces in the planetary life, a strictly cosmic birth, as free from miracle or catastrophe as the coming of an infant into the world or the transformation of the earth in spring ; in a word, ' as natural as the visible known course of things.' [1]

"You will observe that this is a mere scientific hypothesis, and not a religious dogma. I have carefully excluded from it any theological, metaphysical, or even ethical opinions which might seem to prejudice it in your eyes. You may have your own opinions upon such points, and the argument will still hold. You may picture yourself as the merest combination of atoms that the materialist can conceive ; but I have shown you that the dissolution of our gross organized bodies ' would not be our destruction, even without determining whether our living substances be material or immaterial.' You may imagine that combination of your atoms to have been as fortuitous as

[1] Butler's *Analogy*, chap. i.

any that the atheist can trace; but 'that we are to live hereafter is just as reconcilable with the scheme of atheism, and as well to be accounted for by it, as that we are now alive is; and therefore nothing can be more absurd than to argue, from that scheme, that there can be no future state.' You may even discard the moral motives of such a state for any humane virtues that the secularist can practice, as 'if it were certain that our future interest no way depended upon our present behavior;' yet 'curiosity could not but sometimes bring a subject in which we may be so highly interested to our thoughts, especially upon the mortality of others or the near prospect of our own;' and it is in the light of such mere curiosity, as a question of pure science, that I have put it before you, to be tested as coolly as you would dissect an embryo or a chrysalis."

Lucretius, if history speaks truly, was not the man to shirk a question because of its logical consequences, and we can fancy without much effort what sort of rejoinder a true Lucretian would make to the Bishop's reasoning.

"I have listened," he might say, "to your ingenious argument with the interest of a philosopher. It bears upon a subject which engrossed some of the finest minds of Greece and Rome, from Socrates and Plato to Cicero and Seneca. It was not, you are aware, the doctrine of Epicurus, nor that which I learned from my master. He taught me that from atoms all things have come, and to atoms they must return. Through their endless compositions and decompositions the forms of man, beast, bird, and flower appear and disappear, come and go, and are seen no more. Even the ethereal and luminous particles of the soul itself, together with the grosser body through which they are diffused, must scatter and vanish like down before the wind. Death is therefore the mere dissolution of certain compounded atoms which thenceforth can serve no higher purpose than to enrich the earth and nourish plants and animals which may feed other generations of men.

"And this theory he framed into eloquent verse, as I have told you, for the very purpose of counteracting certain dogmas which dominated in his time. He saw men everywhere terrified with omens and disasters, which they attributed to the anger of the gods, and in order to dispel their fears, depicted those ideal beings in a remote heaven of apathy, sublimely indifferent to mortals, while nature moved on beneath, with her measureless surges of atoms, majestically as the roll of his own hexameter. He found his countrymen wasting their best days in alternate dread and hope of Tartarean torments and Elysian raptures, and admonished them that the truest and highest virtue would scorn such selfish motives, and only look for the reward of duty in a tranquil enjoyment of the present life. And that other remaining terror of death which was ever shading their path he stripped before them into an empty negation as the mere loss of life, the last atomic thrill with which to glide into the passionless calm of the gods. He lived about sixty years before the Christian era. As I have explained to you, he died in the faith in which he had lived, and by his own tragic fate illustrated his creed as he stood, in the prime of life, at the height of his fame, about to execute that purpose from which the more irresolute Hamlet quailed : —

> " ' And therefore now
> Let her, that is the womb and tomb of all,
> Great Nature, take, and forcing far apart
> Those blind beginnings that have made me man,
> Dash them anew together at her will
> Through all her cycles.' [1]

Now I do not say, I have not said, that I adopt these theological and ethical opinions of my master, though they were essential parts of his system ; but if I should lay them aside, as you have laid aside yours, there would then remain this mere hypothesis before us to be tested like any other by the facts. And it strikes me simply as a strong physical analogy

[1] Tennyson's *Lucretius*.

which still lacks confirmation. Let me show you how far I might go with you. You have proved that death may be but the birth into another life, that there is nothing improbable in a future state into which we may pass 'just as naturally as we came into the present.' Seneca surmised as much when he likened those who look for a future life to children in the womb preparing for this world. You have also projected into the future new and higher organic types beyond those which, from the mollusk up to man, have been unfolded in the past. Such attempted prevision cannot seem wholly unscientific to a Lucretian, who believes it would have been possible 'from a knowledge of the properties of the molecules of the cosmic vapor to have predicted the state of the fauna of Britain in the year 1869 with as much certainty as one can say what will happen to the vapor of the breath on a cold winter's day.'[1] Nor have we any right 'to assume that man's present faculties end the series' which has extended all the way 'from the Iguanodon and his cotemporaries to the President and members of the British Association.'[2] But at this point the difficulties begin. You have not supplied all the intermediate links in your ideal scale between our future and our present or-

[1] Prof. Huxley in *The Academy* for 1870.
[2] Prof. Tyndall's Address at the British Association in 1868.

ganized selves. You have not shown the one evolving out of the other, the higher out of the lower. You have not exhibited that coming psychical body as originating among the spaceless atoms or punctual forces or plastic processes of the present organism, nor exposed to view the germination of its peculiar faculties and powers. You have not proved the capacity of existing earth and man to produce such spiritual bodies. You have not determined whether the interval between them and us will be brief or long; whether they will recover consciousness soon or late; whether they will be developed slowly or in a moment. In a word, the evidences of such a metamorphosis cannot be gathered from the existing state of knowledge, and if immediately forthcoming would appear little short of miraculous. Upon one point, however, we are agreed. You concede to science those rights of unrestricted search and free discussion which have been so hardly won in 'the progress of learning and of liberty.' That is all I ask. And I beg to assure you that in the event of any other trustworthy proofs of a future state being produced, it would be no bar to the theory even in the view of a Lucretian, that it should be found coincident with the Jewish and Christian prejudices of a right reverend prelate whom no one admires more than I do. On the contrary, to receive and act upon it, at least as a working hypothesis, would be but a dictate of Greek wisdom as well as Roman virtue."

LORD BACON AS UMPIRE BETWEEN BISHOP BUTLER AND A LUCRETIAN.

Leaving these somewhat prejudiced opponents, let us now turn to another historic personage, accepted by them and by us all with the concurrent voice of more than two centuries of trial as an umpire, according to the stilted verse of Cowley,

> "Whom a wise king and nature chose
> Lord Chancellor of both their laws."

Francis Bacon was neither a mere scientist nor a mere divine, but a civilian and philosopher who embraced within the view of his judicial intellect the most advanced science and the best divinity of his time. He projected and partly constructed a magnificent "Instauration of the Sciences," which was designed to include all existing knowledge, both divine and human, in one comprehensive system. May we find any decisions of this high authority that will bear upon the controversy?

At one moment, indeed, he seems to lean toward the side of Lucretius. Having spoken of a sensitive or produced soul which he describes as derived from the elements, and common to man and the brutes, he urges more diligent inquiry into its faculties of voluntary motion and sensibility, and as to its nature, distinctly allows it must be material, " a corporeal substance, attenuated by heat and rendered invisible, as a subtile breath or aura, of a flamy and airy nature, diffused through the whole body, but in perfect creatures residing chiefly in the head and thence running through the nerves, being fed and recruited by the spirituous blood of the arteries, as Telesius and his follower Donius have usefully shown."

At another moment his judgment is on the side of Butler. Superadding to the sensitive or produced soul that rational or inspired soul which proceeds from the breath of God and distinguishes man from the brutes, he concludes that " inquiries with relation to its nature, as whether it be native or adventitious, separable or inseparable, mortal or immortal, how far subject to laws of matter, how far not, and the like, — though they might be more thoroughly sifted in philosophy than hitherto they have been, — in the end must be turned over to religion for determination and decision; since no knowledge of the substance of the rational soul can be had from philosophy, but must be derived from the same divine inspiration, whence the substance thereof originally proceeded."

At the same time, he is careful to vindicate such a method of turning the scale by Scriptural authority as still consistent and just to both parties: "We would not have borrowed this division from divinity, had it not also agreed with philosophy. For there are many excellencies of the human soul above the souls of brutes, manifest even to those who philosophize only according to sense. And wherever so many and such great excellencies are found, a specific difference should always be made. We do not, therefore, approve that confused and promiscuous manner of the philosophers in treating the functions of the soul, as if the soul of man differed in degree rather than species from the soul of brutes, as the sun differs from the stars, or gold from other metals."

And this is but an example of the general manner in which the great acknowledged master of philosophy would treat that whole class of scientific and religious problems which we have described as connected with the origin, course, and destiny of nature.

Now, he yields to science all it can claim, as he argues so eloquently that the inquiry for final causes is wrongly placed in physics, and hath made a great devastation in that province: "And, therefore, the natural philosophies of Democritus and others, who allow no God or mind in the frame of things, but attribute the structure of the universe to infinite essays and trials of nature, or what they call fate or fortune, and assign the causes of particular things to the necessity of matter without any intermixture of final causes, seem, so far as we can judge from the remains of their philosophy, much more solid, and to have gone deeper into nature, with regard to physical causes, than the philosophy of Aristotle or Plato; and this only because they never meddled with final causes, which the others were perpetually inculcating."

Again, he reserves for religion all that it demands, while he shows that final causes, when kept where they belong within the bounds of theology and metaphysics, are not repugnant to physical causes, but agree excellently with them as expressing the intentions of Providence in the consequences of nature: "But Democritus and Epicurus when they advanced their atoms were thus far tolerated by some, but when they asserted the fabric of all things to be raised by a fortuitous concourse of these atoms, without the help of mind, they became universally ridiculous. So far are physical causes from drawing men off from God and Providence, that on the contrary, the philosophers employed in discovering them can find no rest but by flying to God and Providence at last."

And when we inquire how these two adjacent provinces are to be preserved and adjusted, we may hear him discoursing of a Primary Philosophy, or mother of all the sciences, by whom they are to be cherished, and around whom their wrangling sisterhood is to be gathered in harmony. His conception of such a philosophy may seem crude and vague, but not more so than might have been expected in that age. In fact he is inclined to note it as still wanting; and in terms that almost exactly describe the exigency upon us at this hour: "For I find a certain rhapsody of natural theology, logic, and physics, delivered in a certain sublimity of discourse, by such as aim at being admired for standing on the pinnacles of the sciences; but what we mean is, without ambition, to design some general science, for the reception of axioms, not peculiar to any one science, but common to a number of them."[1]

THE UMPIRAGE OF PHILOSOPHY.

The three personages before us have thus illustrated the classes to which they respectively belong, and the interests which they represent. Philosophy, in the best sense of the word, is the umpire between Science and Religion. As originally defined by Pythagoras and Cicero, it is itself the science of things divine and human, together with their causes. As that academic faculty which is complementary to the faculties of law, medicine, and theol-

[1] Bacon's *Advancement of Learning*, book iii., chap. 4.

ogy, it includes whatsoever is common to both the secular and sacred departments of learning. As the science of knowledge, it aims to ascertain inductively the validity, the limits and the functions of reason and revelation, the two great correlate factors of knowledge. As the science of the absolute, so called by the Germans, it takes within its scope both the finite and the infinite, both the knowable and the unknowable, for the respective provinces of reason and revelation. As that summary universal science of which Bacon speaks, to which all the rest are tributary, it receives and cherishes impartially and equally the discovered and the revealed bodies of knowledge, that it may organize them into a rational system. And finally, in the most common and literal sense of the word, as the love of wisdom, Philosophy, while including and fostering the scientific virtues of curiosity, accuracy, and candor together with the religious graces of reverence, humility, and faith, over and above these qualities retains others more peculiar to herself, such as that power of abstraction, that insight into reality, that catholicity of view, that unquenchable craving for unity of truth and symmetry of knowledge, which are not so likely to be practiced by the mere scientist or the mere religionist, so long as he is immersed in his own special researches, and which yet easily come to them both the moment they step into her wider sphere.

It is to be regretted that a prejudice should exist in some minds against a word of such noble significance, and all the more as it is only in rare cases that its true meaning would be repudiated. Though a few scientists and religionists may now and then have denounced philosophy as mystical or rationalistic, yet the great mass would simply resent the imputation of being unphilosophical, as an insult to their understandings. There is plainly a good and valuable sense of the term which both parties spontaneously unite in using, and which ought not to be sacrificed in any mere logomachy, so long us we have no better word to express it. If we would characterize a lover, seeker and reconciler of all truths, both natural and revealed, we must term him a philosopher. If we would describe that special work which is to be done in adjusting the relations of religion and science, in ascertaining and defending their respective spheres and prerogatives, in devising and applying logical rules to their pending controversies, in sifting their several portions of truth from error, and combining them into a harmonious system — we can only speak of all this as a peculiar intellectual task belonging neither to religion alone, nor to science alone, but to their common ally and friend, philosophy.

Philosophy, at least, is the actual, the accepted umpire. The two parties have ever in fact, even though without concert, practically owned her jurisdiction, and sought to justify themselves to each other in her view. It has been their aim to show that in being scientific or religious they mean to be also philosophical, to sacrifice no essential portion of the whole truth, and do no outrage to that common reason without which we can judge neither of the evidence of religion, nor of the claims of science. Instinctively they have appealed to her, in every great crisis of free thought, to guard and vindicate at once the authority of revelation and the rights of reason. And this unconscious tribute has been more than repaid. To her, from the days of Justin, the first apologist, Religion largely owes its evidences, its defenses, its appliances; to her, since the time of Aristotle, the first great logician, Science is mainly indebted for its methods, its rights, its triumphs; and at this moment, in spite of their conflicting partisans, under her mild umpirage, whatsoever the one can establish as truly revealed, and the other as actually discovered, will be spontaneously accepted by them both.

Philosophy, too, is the only available umpire. If we wished it otherwise we would wish in vain. The moment the two parties come into collision, it is found that neither can impose its own terms upon the other. Paramount as Religion must be in her own sphere with her inspired Bible and her illumined Church, yet scientific men will not accept from mere religionists, as such, a judgment upon their theories; and paramount as Science must be in her own sphere, with her unerring methods and unquestionable facts, yet religious men will not accept from mere scientists a judgment upon their doctrines. Neither party will be acknowledged as a competent and disinterested judge of the questions in dispute. Neither can afford from its own one-sided position a calm and full survey of the whole field of controversy. The rival claimants must leave their different spheres, though without sacrificing them, and for the time at least appear in some middle outside province which shall be equally removed from their respective prejudices and temptations, and where the whole truth shall be sought and prized as truth alone; and for such a province we have no better name than philosophy. If at that only possible tribunal either could prevail against the other, so far as we can see (without some miraculous interposition for which we have no right to look), religion would degenerate into superstition and science into imbecility; but being there legitimated and reconciled, they will join hands as twin daughters of God and lovers of man.

Philosophy, moreover, has become the one desirable umpire. It is best that the two parties should agree to treat the mixed problems rising between them as properly philosophical, rather than merely scientific or purely religious. Their attempts to settle them apart, each by its own method, have brought upon us overwhelming evils. If the time once was when the religious class was unfolding a whole cyclopedia of science out of the Scriptures, from Genesis to the Apocalypse, as pure dogma and mystery of faith, yet the time has now come when a few, at least, in the scientific class are exhibiting a new genesis and apocalypse of religion as the sheer product of science and speculation. And it is high time — I venture to say in the name of the great body of sober and fair minds on both sides, who refuse to commit themselves to such wild extremes — that the two antagonists, on thus emerging from their respective provinces into the broad plain of philosophy, should learn to respect their common rights and interests, and not imagine that either can claim the whole field against the other. It is time that the religionist should recognize before him an immense mass of discovered facts, theories, hypotheses which are the fruit of two thousand years of research, which stand upon foundations of proof that cannot be shaken and are rising into a superstructure of knowledge too vast even to be conceived. It is time, too, that the scientist should cease to ignore that vast body of truths, doctrines, dogmas, backed by evidences which have been accumulating for eighteen centuries under the most searching criticism, which have more than convinced the great master minds of the past, and which are mounting every hour with cumulative probability toward moral certainty itself. And when at length both parties meet face to face, as they are now meeting, before the final problem of the universe, it is time for the one to admit that the processes of creation have not been revealed and cannot, by the most exact criticism, the most profound exegesis, the most systematic divinity, ever be discerned in the mere letter of Holy Scripture, and for the other to perceive that the theory of a Creator, anthropomorphic as it may appear, still keeps the field, still satisfies an immense number of scientific minds, and is not likely to be abandoned even by the most advanced scientists, until something else or something better has been offered in its place. Only when they have thus taken philosophical views of the whole range of knowledge will they cease their raids upon each other's territory, and no longer maintain hostile barriers or hollow truces within the domain of truth. In the realm of Philosophy alone can they meet and find their needed mutual support, completion, and harmony.

The reconciliation of Science and Religion is not only a distinctive problem of Philosophy, but precisely that one chief problem by the solution of which her own function is exhausted, her goal attained, her mission accomplished. In establishing the validity of human reason, in maintaining the authority of divine revelation, in logically combining them as coördinate means of knowledge and pouring their blended light upon all classes of facts, she is but fulfilling that sublime ideal towards which her followers from age to age have been struggling with unquenchable hope and courage. The one last perfect Philosophy is to be sought and can only be found in the demonstrated harmony of Science and Religion.

THE TRUE PHILOSOPHICAL SPIRIT.

It may be well to say at this point that no disparagement of any one of the three interests, certainly no exaltation of Science over Religion or of Philosophy over either, is implied in this definition of their related provinces. An umpire is but the servant of the game that he watches, making neither the laws nor the facts, but simply applying the one to the other. And that only true Philosophy which seeks to embrace both Science and Religion in their normal relations must itself be predetermined and limited by them. Any attempt of the philosophic spirit to intrude into their domains with the view of distorting scientific facts or religious truths for mere speculative purposes, can only issue in confusion and evil. The so-called philosophies of Nature, such as those of Schelling and Oken, which aim to construct hypothetically the material universe without full empirical research, as well as the miscalled philosophies of religion, such as those of Hegel and Comte, which seek to prejudge the powers and relations of the Absolute Intelligence regardless of its actual expressions, are alike vain attempts of the mere reason to dispense with experience and revelation. And the would-be philosophers who aspire to conciliate the scientific and the religious spirit without any practical acquaintance with either are only sure to fall under the contempt of both.

As little would it follow from the proposed definition, that the philosophical spirit must needs be organized in some visible tribunal, issuing authoritative decisions. The scientific spirit does not thus reach its results through any of the mere institutions or associations which embody and express it; and the religious spirit, though incorporated in churches and councils and claiming the authority of an infallible Scripture, does not command universal agreement. It is the crowning misfortune of the present crisis, that neither the disciples of

Religion nor the votaries of Science are united in their respective interpretations of the Bible and of Nature, but appear divided among themselves, as well as opposed to each other, by endless hypotheses and dogmas, throughout the entire field of research. And yet, as there must still be such a thing as true science and true religion amid all the schools and the sects, so there may be a true philosophy ever discriminating and mediating between them and a hidden fraternity of philosophers more or less consciously striving to bring them into harmony.

It seems scarcely necessary to add that there can be no invidious distinction of classes in the pure democracy of intellect. The philosophic class is but recruited from the scientific and religious ranks, and can neither exist nor flourish without them. Any one joins it who pleases, stays in it as long as he chooses, and falls or rises by his own merit. None need to enter it who feel, as at times we all feel, that life is full enough of problems without adding to their number. Some may prefer to seclude themselves within their own provinces, to which they are wedded with the zeal of a votary. Others may make chance excursions beyond only to return as quickly to less debatable ground. Still others may even accept conscious contradiction rather than open conflict, resolutely holding the sternest creed with the strictest science, like the great Faraday, of whose laboratory and oratory it has been said, that he never entered either without shutting the door of the other. But the days for such a state of parties seem to be passing away. The trumpet of a new campaign has been sounded. Combatants have been marshaled and the lines are forming. When scientific and religious bodies have already begun to discuss the same problems from their opposite points of view, there can only be warfare or agreement. And in such a crisis, it is easy to see that the honors are more likely to go to those who are championing the extreme wings of Philosophy than to any that may be so brave or so rash as to risk the cross fire between them.

AN ILLUSTRATIVE PHILOSOPHICAL SCHEME FOR HARMONIZING SCIENCE AND RELIGION.

It may give this discussion more definiteness and point, and rescue it from any vague generality otherwise resting upon it, to sketch in outline a scheme of such philosophical principles as have been advocated — not, of course, with any hope of settling the problems before us, still less of issuing final rules for their settlement, but simply as an illustration of the field which has been defined and the work which yet remains to be performed. Such a scheme, it is obvious, will labor under the great disadvantage of appearing as a mere dry, abstruse statement, when viewed apart from the facts and reasonings which support it.

If we arrange the sciences upon the only philosophical principle, according to the order of facts in space and time as coexistent and successive, we shall have a series, rising from the simplest physical to the most complex psychical phenomena, and embracing both the celestial and terrestrial divisions of each set of phenomena, the mechanical, chemical, and organical; the individual, social, and religious. And by still further separating them into abstract and concrete groups, we shall get for our working classification that one which has been produced in this paper, including in itself the physical sciences of astronomy, geology, and anthropology, and the psychical sciences of psychology, sociology, and theology. This will be our map of science, spread out before us with its bounded provinces and its known and unknown regions.

	Abstract Sciences.	*Concrete Sciences.*	
Celestial and Terrestrial.	{ Religious. Social. Individual. Organical. Chemical. Mechanical.	Theology. Sociology. Psychology. Anthropology. Geology. Astronomy.	} Psychical. } Physical.

Assuming, as the result of a course of inductive logic (which cannot here be detailed), that reason and revelation are the two great factors of knowledge, we shall then have the task of devising the axioms or logical canons for their correlation in the different provinces of research which have been defined and characterized. They can only be obtained by combined reasoning and research, and will naturally fall into three classes, according as we study the normal, the existing, and the prospective state of the sciences.

The Normal State of the Sciences.

1. In each science reason and revelation are complemental factors of knowledge, the former discovering what the latter has not revealed and the latter revealing what the former cannot discover.

2. In the ascending scale of the sciences the province of reason contracts as that of revelation expands, with the growing complexity, obscurity, and human importance of the sciences themselves.

3. The joint action of reason and revelation throughout the sciences logically involves the perfectibility of knowledge or the indefinite expansion of science toward omniscience.

The Existing State of the Sciences.

1. Hypotheses and dogmas are to be formed by the scientist and religionist independently,

each in his own province, and by his own methods.

2. Dogmas within the province of the scientist must be tested in the same manner as his own hypotheses; and hypotheses within the province of the religionist, in the same manner as his own dogmas.

3. Conflicting hypotheses and dogmas can only be provisionally adjusted by exhibiting the problem of opinion, according as reason or revelation predominates in the normal scale of the sciences.

The Prospective State of the Sciences.

1. In the progress of the sciences, conflicting hypotheses and dogmas, by their own attritions and mutual corrections, pass into the theories and creeds accepted by both parties.

2. This gradual conversion of the hypothetical and dogmatic into the scientific, proceeds in the order of the sciences, from one set of facts to another, from the simple to the complex, from the lower to the higher, from the physical through the psychical sciences.

3. The historical goal of the whole scientific process, ever to be approached even if never attained, is the absorption of positive in absolute science or perfect knowledge.

THE FUTURE OF KNOWLEDGE THUS HARMONIZED.

A glimpse is enough to show us the vastness of the theme. Not by any one mind, not by any one people, not by any one age can it be mastered. It is the mighty argument of successive generations, proceeding with stately steps from its premises in a remote past toward its conclusions in a distant future. If we will surrender ourselves to it we can see whither it is carrying us, and exult in the prospect.

In the view of Religion everything may appear miraculous; in the view of Science everything may appear natural; while in the view of Philosophy both will only appear more and more consistent aspects of one and the same reality. Let Science, if it can, resolve the whole course of nature into one continuous process of correlate forces; let Religion, if it must, exhibit that course of nature as one dazzling series of miracles; a true Philosophy will yet behold them blending together as but the sure logic and even pulse of one Almighty Mind, ever reasoning through the whole creation, and flushing with life all creatures.

As yet, indeed, to us who can see but a speck, a span, of the two vast coinciding spheres, they must seem confused, dark and often contradictory. But " there may be beings in the universe, whose capacities and knowledge and views may be so extensive as that the whole Christian dispensation may to them appear natural; as natural as the visible known course of things appears to us." Be that as it may, if we will read the future as we can read the past, it will not seem incredible that the most extreme investigators are now but groping through the darkness toward some central point where, at length, they shall meet as in a focus of light. Only, we may be sure, they will meet there, not like those two rash knights at their first encounter, not like those eager champions who are now filling the air with challenges and criminations, but rather like exhausted and bleeding warriors, after having fought their way into a recognition of each other's truth and virtue, to clasp hands as friends who had but mistaken themselves for foes.

SYNOPSIS.

HISTORICAL ORIGIN OF THE SCHISM BETWEEN RELIGION AND SCIENCE.

CONSEQUENT EXISTING STATE OF THE SCIENCES :
  Numerous Unsolved Problems ;
  Scientific Hypotheses and Religious Dogmas.

PROBLEMS IN ASTRONOMY, WITH HYPOTHESES AND DOGMAS :
  Primitive Evolution of Suns and Planets ;
  Instantaneous Creation of the Heavens.
  Plurality of Uninhabited Worlds ;
  Hierarchy of the Heavenly Hosts.
  Ultimate Dissolution of Planets and Suns ;
  Miraculous Renewal of the Heavens and Earth.

PROBLEMS IN GEOLOGY, WITH HYPOTHESES AND DOGMAS :
  Secular Formation of Strata, Floras, and Faunas ;
  Successive Creations in Six Days.
  Ultimate Cooling of the Globe ;
  Predicted Renovation by Fire.
  Periodic Changes of Climate and Species ;
  Judgments of the Deluge and the Conflagration.

PROBLEMS IN ANTHROPOLOGY, WITH HYPOTHESES AND DOGMAS :
  Development of Animal into Human Species ;
  Creation of Adam in the Divine Image.
  Gradual Rise of Races, Languages, and Arts ;
  Miraculous Confusion and Dispersion at Babel.
  Physical Decline of the Future Human Race ;
  Predicted Renewal of Man with the Earth.

PROBLEMS IN THE PSYCHICAL SCIENCES : PSYCHOLOGY, SOCIOLOGY, AND THEOLOGY :
  Production and Dissolution of the Mind ;
  Creation and Regeneration of the Soul.

{ Natural Growth and Decay of Societies;
Supernatural Career of the Church.
Progressive Scale of Natural Religions;
Predicted Triumph of Revealed Religion.

PROBLEMS IN METAPHYSICAL SCIENCE:

{ Phenomenal Nature of Mind and Matter;
Pre-ordained Harmony of Soul and Body.
Development of the World from Absolute Reason and Force;
Creation of the World by the Father through the Son.

PROBLEMS IN THE SCIENCE OF THE SCIENCES:

{ Destruction of Theology by Positive Science;
Rectification of Science by a Divine Revelation.
The Goal of Science in Absolute Nescience;
The Beatific Vision and New Apocalypse.

PHILOSOPHICAL NATURE OF ALL THESE PROBLEMS:

They are not exclusively Scientific;
They are not exclusively Religious;
They are partly Scientific and partly Religious.

PROFESSOR TYNDALL'S ILLUSTRATION OF ONE OF THESE PROBLEMS:

Renewed Argument of Bishop Butler;
Rejoinder of a Lucretian;
Lord Bacon as Umpire.

THE UMPIRAGE OF PHILOSOPHY BETWEEN SCIENCE AND RELIGION.

Definition of Philosophy;
Philosophy the Accepted Umpire;
Philosophy the only Available Umpire;
Philosophy the one Desirable Umpire.

THE FINAL PHILOSOPHY TO BE SOUGHT IN THE LOGICAL RECONCILIATION OF SCIENCE AND RELIGION.

THE TRUE PHILOSOPHICAL SPIRIT:

It intrudes neither into Science nor into Religion;
It mediates by no mere visible Authority;
It is itself only recruited from the ranks of both Science and Religion.

A Philosophical Scheme for Harmonizing Science and Revealed Religion:
    The Sciences inductively Classified.
    The Normal State of the Sciences.
    The Existing State of the Sciences.
    The Prospective State of the Sciences.
The Future of Knowledge thus Harmonized.

POPULAR AND STANDARD WORKS
PUBLISHED BY
SCRIBNER, ARMSTRONG & CO.
NEW YORK.
In 1874.

AGASSIZ'S (PROF. LOUIS) Structure of Animal Life. *Illus.* 8vo.... ...$1.50

BIBLE COMMENTARY. Vol. IV. Embracing Job, Psalms, Proverbs, Ecclesiastes and Song of Solomon. 8vo.................................... 5.00

BLACKIE'S (PROF. J. S.) Self-Culture. 16mo. *Fifth Thousand*.......... 1.00

BUSHNELL'S (DR. H.) Forgiveness and Law. 12mo.... .... 1.75

THE BRIC-A-BRAC SERIES. Edited by RICHARD HENRY STODDARD. 1. Chorley, Planche, and Young. 2. Thackeray and Dickens. 3. Merimee, Lamartine, and Sand. 4. Barham, Harness, and Hodder. 5. The Greville Memoirs. 6. Personal Reminiscences by Moore and Jerdan. 7. Personal Reminiscences by Cornelia Knight and Thomas Raikes. Each 1 vol. Square 12mo. Cloth................................... 1.50

CHRISTLIEB'S (PROF. THEO.) Modern Doubt and Christian Belief. 8vo. 3.00

CURTIUS' (PROF. DR. ERNST) History of Greece. Vol. IV. and Vol. V. *Completing the Work, with Index.* Crown 8vo. Each................. 2.50

DODGE'S (MRS. MARY MAPES) Rhymes and Jingles. *Illustrated.* Square 12mo... 3.00

EPOCHS OF HISTORY. 1. The Era of the Protestant Revolution. 2. The Crusades. 3. The Thirty Years' War, 1618–1648. 4. The Houses of Lancaster and York. Each one vol. 16mo, *with outline Maps.* Price, per vol. in cloth.. 1.00

FROUDE'S English in Ireland in 18th Century. Vols. II. and III. *Completing the Work.* Crown 8vo. Each................. .... 2.50

HODGE'S (DR. CHAS.) What is Darwinism? 12mo........................ 1.50

HOLLAND'S (DR J. G.) Mistress of the Manse. *A Poem.* 12mo......... 1.50

HURST'S (DR. J. F.) Life and Literature in the Fatherland. Crown 8vo.... 2.25

LANGE'S COMMENTARY. The Minor Prophets. Revelation. Job. Edited by Dr. P. SCHAFF. 8vo. Each............................. 5.00

MARCOY'S Travels in South America. *Profusely Illustrated.* 2 vols....15.00

MARSH (G. P.) The Earth as Modified by Human Action. 8vo............. 4.50

MULLER (PROF. MAX) On Missions. 8vo................................. 1.00

MURRAY'S (PROF. A. S.) Manual of Mythology. *Illustrated.* Crown 8vo. 2.25

PARKER'S (DR. JOSEPH) The Paraclete. 8vo............................. 2.00

ROGERS' (HENRY) Superhuman Origin of the Bible. 12mo................ 2.00

SAINTINE'S (X. B.) Myths of the Rhyne. *Illustrated by G. Doré.* Quarto.10.00

STANLEY'S (H. M.) How I Found Livingstone. *A New and Cheap Edition*.. 3.50

TORREY'S (PROF. JOSEPH) Theory of Fine Art. 12mo................... 1.50

VAN OOSTERZEE'S (DR. J. J.) Christian Dogmatics. 2 vols. 8vo........ 6.00

VERNE'S (JULES) Meridiana. *Illustrated.* 12mo. Cloth. *Eleventh Thousand.* 75c. A Journey to the Centre of the Earth. *Illustrated.* 12mo. Cloth. 75c. Floating City and Blockade Runners. *Illustrated.* 12mo. Cloth. *Fourth Thousand.* $3.00. Mysterious Island, Wrecked in the Air. *Illustrated.* 12mo. Cloth. *Thirteenth Thousand.* 60c. Stories of Adventure (Comprising "Meridiana," and "Journey to the Centre of the Earth.") *Cheap Edition.* Illustrated. 12mo. Cloth 1.50

WHITNEY'S (PROF. W. D.) Oriental and Linguistic Studies. SECOND SERIES. Crown 8vo.. 2.50

WOOLSEY'S (DR. T. D.) International Law. *New Edition.* Crown 8vo... 2.50

*** *Any of the above books sent pre-paid to any address upon receipt of the price by the Publishers.*

An Important Historical Series.

EPOCHS OF HISTORY.

EDITED BY

EDWARD E. MORRIS, M.A.,

Each 1 vol. 16mo. with Outline Maps. Price per volume, in cloth, $1.00.

HISTORIES of countries are rapidly becoming so numerous that it is almost impossible for the most industrious student to keep pace with them. Such works are, of course, still less likely to be mastered by those of limited leisure. It is to meet the wants of this very numerous class of readers that the *Epochs of History* has been projected. The series will comprise a number of compact, handsomely printed manuals, prepared by thoroughly competent hands, each volume complete in itself, and sketching succinctly the most important epochs in the world's history, always making the history of a nation subordinate to this more general idea. No attempt will be made to recount all the events of any given period. The aim will be to bring out in the clearest light the salient incidents and features of each epoch. Special attention will be paid to the literature, manners, state of knowledge, and all those characteristics which exhibit the life of a people as well as the policy of their rulers during any period. To make the text more readily intelligible, outline maps will be given with each volume, and where this arrangement is desirable they will be distributed throughout the text so as to be more easy of reference. A series of works based upon this general plan can not fail to be widely useful in popularizing history as science has lately been popularized. Those who have been discouraged from attempting more ambitious works because of their magnitude, will naturally turn to these *Epochs of History* to get a general knowledge of any period; students may use them to great advantage in refreshing their memories and in keeping the true perspective of events, and in schools they will be of immense service as text books,—a point which shall be kept constantly in view in their preparation.

THE FOLLOWING VOLUMES ARE NOW READY:

THE ERA OF THE PROTESTANT REVOLUTION. By F. SEEBOHM, Author of "The Oxford Reformers—Colet, Erasmus, More," with appendix by P-of. GEO. P. FISHER, of Yale College. Author of "HISTORY OF THE REFORMATION."

The CRUSADES. By Rev. G. W. Cox, M.A , Author of the "History of Greece."

The THIRTY YEARS' WAR, 1618—1648. By SAMUEL RAWSON GARDINER.

THE HOUSES OF LANCASTER AND YORK; with the CONQUEST and LOSS of FRANCE. By JAMES GAIRDNER of the Public Record Office. *Now ready.*

THE FRENCH REVOLUTION AND FIRST EMPIRE: an Historical Sketch. By WILLIAM O'CONNOR MORRIS, with an appendix by Hon. ANDREW D. WHITE, President of Cornell University.

☞ *Copies sent post-paid, on receipt of price, by the Publishers.*

www.ingramcontent.com/pod-product-compliance
Lightning Source LLC
Chambersburg PA
CBHW020240090426
42735CB00010B/1778